ECCENTRIC
Epitaphs
GAFFES FROM BEYOND THE GRAVE

Let's talk of graves, of worms and epitaphs ...

William Shakespeare, *Richard II*

This edition published by Barnes & Noble, Inc,
by arrangement with Michelle Lovric
2000 Barnes & Noble Books
ISBN 0-7607-2198-X

Eccentric Epitaphs by Michelle Lovric
Designed by Lisa Pentreath and Michelle Lovric
copyright © 2000 Michelle Lovric, Covent Garden, London
Editorial Assistant: Kristina Blagojevitch
Printed in China by Imago

0 9 8 7 6 5 4 3 2 1

ACKNOWLEDGEMENTS
The editor gratefully acknowledges the help of Iain Campbell in
picture research for this book, and thanks to Joanna Skepers for
her help and inspiration in all things, particularly these.

CEASE TO LAMENT
HIS CHANGE, YE JUST,
HE'S ONLY GONE
FROM DUST TO DUST.

ECCENTRIC
Epitaphs

Gaffes
FROM BEYOND THE GRAVE

edited by
Michelle Lovric

BARNES
&NOBLE
BOOKS
NEW YORK

There is a certain frame of mind to which a
cemetery is, if not an antidote, at least an
alleviation. If you are in a fit of the
blues, go nowhere else.

Robert Louis Stevenson, *Immortelles*

EDITOR'S NOTE

Anyone who visits a churchyard will be drawn to read the
mossy inscriptions carved into the ancient tombstones.
Epitaphs have always given food for reflection: they serve
not merely to record the death of an individual but to
remind us all of our ultimate fate.

As Samuel Butler wrote:
Our noblest piles and stateliest rooms,
Are mere out-houses to our tombs;
Cities, tho' ere so great and brave,
But mere warehouses to the grave.

We have been erecting inscribed monuments to our dead
since the dawn of writing. The first tomb is recorded in
Genesis. The writing of epitaphs has always been an art.
The requisite combination of wit and brevity has appealed
to writers, some of whom, by the 17th century, had taken
to composing mock-epitaphs of living public figures and
friends. By the 18th century it had become a popular
pastime to collect epitaphs, particularly curious and
amusing ones. The sentimental Victorian period saw a
flowering of anthologies of epitaphs: huge tomes with
names such as *Gleanings from God's Acre* were popular.

Some of these epitaphs are apocryphal. Some writers
have pre-empted their loved ones by writing their own
epitaphs. Sadly, many of the original gravestones and even
some churchyards no longer exist: what has survived is
only the memory of them in the communities where they
once were.

A piece of a Churchyard fits everybody.

George Herbert, *Iacula Prudentum*

CONTENTS

Stop, Traveller

STOP TRAVELLER

Once I Wasn't.
Then I Was.
Now I ain't Again.

Lee County, Mississippi

Memento Mori

JOHN LINNING
(DIED 1824)

Stop, reader! stop and view this stone,
   And ponder well where I am gone.
      Then, pondering,
         take thou home
            this rhyme —
               The grave next
               opened may be thine.

Devon

AMEN

SHALL WEE ALL DIE?
WEE SHALL DIE ALL.
ALL DIE SHALL WE?
DIE ALL WE SHALL.

Cunwallow, near Helstone, Cornwall

6

MARY RICHARDS
(1740—71)

All ye who stop to read this stone
Consider how soon she was gone.
Death doth not always warning give
Therefore be careful how you live.

St Mary, Doddington

A WARNING ON JOHN WARNER
(DIED 1641, AGED 92)

I WARNER once was to myself
Now Warning am to thee
Both living, dying, dead I was,
See then thou warned be.

St Mary Key, Ipswich, Suffolk

J. N.
(DIED 1678)

Seek not to learn who underneath doth lie.
Learn something more important:
— learn to die.

VISCOUNT CASTLEREAGH
(1769—1822)

Posterity will ne'er survey
A nobler grave than this:
Here lie the bones of Castlereagh:
Stop, traveller, and piss.

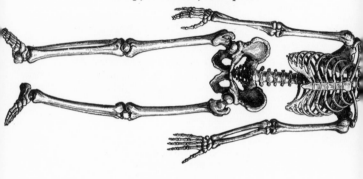

ON A MAN WHO HAD
A REMARKABLY WIDE MOUTH

Here lies a man, as God shall me save,
Whose mouth was wide, as is his grave;
Reader, tread lightly o'er his sod,
For, if he gapes, you're gone, by G—d.

Coleshill, Warwickshire

Stop, reader! I have left a world,
    In which there was a world to do;
Fretting and stewing to be rich —
    Just such a fool as you.

London

Sturdy Oak

Fear God,
Keep the commandments, and
Don't attempt to climb a tree,
For that's what caused the death of me.

Eastwell churchyard, Kent

**ON A MAIDEN LADY
WHO HAD ONCE BEEN JILTED**

Here lies the body of one
    Who died of constancy alone.
Stranger! advance with steps courageous,
For this disease is not contagious.

from Diprose's Book of Epitaphs: Humourous, Eccentric,
Ancient and Remarkable, 1841

Mortal Remains

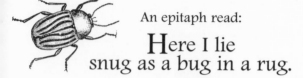

An epitaph read:

Here I lie
snug as a bug in a rug.

An envious relative instructed that he be buried in an adjoining grave with the following inscription above him:

Here I lie
snugger than
that other bugger.

**ROBERT, COMMONLY CALLED BONE PHILIP,
WHO DIED JULY 27TH, 1793,
AGED 63 YEARS**

Here I lie at the Chancel door.
Here I lie because I'm poor.
The further in the more you'll pay.
Here lie I as warm as they.

Kingsbridge, Devon
A similar stone is to be found at Dawlish, Devon

Here lies Matthew Mudd,
   Death did him no hurt;
When alive he was Mudd
And now he's dead he's but dirt.

Walton, Norfolk

Joe Crump, musician
   Once ruddy and plump,
   But now a pale lump,
   Beneath this soft clump,
   Lies honest JOE CRUMP.

ON A CELEBRATED LONDON COOK

Peas to his Hashes;
meaning of course,
Peace to his ashes.

JOHN FLIN, PAINTER
(DIED AGED 67)

Here lies John Flin,
To worms a kin ...

Galway, Ireland

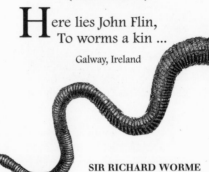

SIR RICHARD WORME
(DIED 1589)

Does worm eat Worme? ...

Peterborough Cathedral, Cambridgeshire

ON AN OLD MAID

Here lies the body of Martha Dias,
Who was always uneasy
and not over pious;
She liv'd to the age of threescore and ten,
And gave that to the worms
she refus'd to the men.

Shrewsbury churchyard, Shropshire

12

Here lies the body of Jonathan Ground,
Who was lost at sea and never found.

Ireland

Here lies the body
of Jonathan Stout.
He fell in the water
and never got out,
And still is supposed
to be floating about.

Connecticut

IN MEMORY OF CAPTAIN UNDERWOOD
WHO WAS DROWNED

Here lies free from blood and slaughter,
Once Underwood — now Underwater.

Sussex

U nderneath this pile of stones
Lies all that's left of Sally Jones.
Her name was Lord, it was not Jones
But Jones was used to rhyme with stones.

Skaneateles, New York

**DOCTOR WALKER, AUTHOR OF A BOOK
ENTITLED PARTICLES**

Here lie
Walker's Particles.

ON A CHEMIST

... Full seventy years his EXALTED ESSENCE
Was HERMETICALLY SEALED in its
TERRENE MATTRASS:
But the RADICAL MOISTURE being EXHAUSTED,
The ELIXIR VITAE spent,
And EXSICCATED TO A CUTICLE,
He could not SUSPEND LONGER in his VEHICLE,
But PRECIPITATED GRADATIM
PER CAMPANAM
To his ORIGINAL DUST.
May the light above, more RESPLENDENT
than BOLOGNAN PHOSPHORUS,
Preserve him from
The ATHANOR, EMPYREUMA,
and REVERBATORY FURNACE
Of the other world,
DEPURATE him from the FAECES and SCORIAE
Of this,
Highly RECTIFY and VOLATILIZE
His ETHEREAL SPIRIT,
Bring it safely over the HELM of human life,
Place it in a PROPER RECIPIENT,
Of CHRISTALLINE ORE,
Among the ELECT of the FLOWERS OF BENJAMIN,
Never to be SATURATED till
The general RESUSCITATION,
DEFLAGRATION, CALCINATION,
and SUBLIMATION
Of all things.

REGRETS – I'VE HAD A FEW

W. C. FIELDS
(1880—1946)

Here lies W. C. Fields.
On the whole
I would rather be living
in Philadelphia.

I poorly lived, I poorly died,
And when I was buried,
nobody cried.

Lillingham, Dorset

H ere lie the remains
of John Hall, Grocer,
The world is not worth a fig,
and I have good raisins for saying so.

Dunmore, Ireland

ALEXANDER THE GREAT
(356—323BC)

Sufficit huic tumulus
Cui non sufficeret obis.
(Here a mound suffices
for one for whom the world
was not large enough.)

Alexander the Great

Dorothy Cecil
unmarried
As yet.

Wimbledon, London

Partridge

MR PARTRIDGE
(DIED 1861)

What! Kill a partridge in the month of May!
Was that done like a sportsman? eh, death, eh?

Ludlow, Shropshire

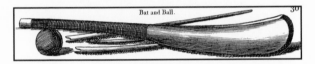

Bat and Ball. 30

ON A CRICKET-PLAYER

I bowl'd, I struck, I caught, I stopp'd —
    Sure life's a game of cricket;
I block'd with care, with caution popp'd,
    Yet Death has hit my wicket.

Churchyard near Salisbury, Wiltshire

GEORGE JOHNSON
Hanged by mistake.

Arizona

18

KING JOSEPH II OF GERMANY
(1741—90)

Here lies Joseph, who was unsuccessful in all his undertakings.

NOTE: The King requested this epitaph for himself.

JOHN KEATS
(1795—1821)

This Grave contains all
that was Mortal of a
YOUNG ENGLISH POET
Who on his Death Bed,
in the Bitterness of his Heart
at the Malicious Power of his enemies,
desired these Words to be engraved
on his Tomb Stone.
"Here lies One
Whose name was writ in Water."

Rome

DOROTHY PARKER
(1893—1967)

Excuse my Dust.

Deadly Sins

ON TWO CHILDREN

Weep not for us, our Parents dear
Nor yet be over sad,
The fewer years we lived on earth
The fewer faults we had.

St Peter's, Palgrave, Suffolk

Stranger weep, for at the age of seven,
Little Willie went to heaven.

(the following lines were added as graffiti)

Cheer up, Stranger, who can tell,
Willie may have gone to hell.

HILAIRE BELLOC
(1870—1953)

When I am dead,
I hope it may be said:
"His sins were scarlet,
but his books were read."

GROUCHO MARX
(1895—1977)

Here lies Groucho Marx
and Lies and Lies and Lies.

P.S. He never kissed an ugly girl.

ON A LIAR

Good passenger!
here lies one here,
That living, did lye every where.

After much eating,
drinking, lying, slandering,
Timocreon of Rhodes
rests here from wandering.

Five letters his life
and death will express,
He scarce knew his A B C,
and he died of X S.

**ON A PERSON
WITH A MOST VORACIOUS APPETITE**

Otho, tomb'd within this glebe so hallow'd,
Had in his life-time many acres swallow'd;
But in return to this voracious limb,
The earth in justice now has swallow'd him.

Here lies Dr Keene, the good Bishop of Chester,
Who eat up a fat goose, but could not digest her.

(18th century)

WILLIAM SIMMONDS
(1673—1753)

Here lies my corpse who was the man
That lov'd a sop in dripping pan
But now believe me I am dead
Now here the pan stands at my head
Still for sop to the last I cry'd
But could not eat and so I died
My neighbours they perhaps may laugh
When they do read my epitaph.

St Mary, Wood Ditton, Gloucestershire

This disease, you ne'er heard tell on —
I died of eating too much melon;
Be careful, then, all you that feed — I
Suffered because I was too greedy.

Chigwell, Essex

ON W. ELDERTON,
RED-NOSED BALLADEER

Dead drunk, here Elderton doth lie;
Dead as he is, he still is dry:
So of him it may well be said,
Here he, but not his thirst, is laid.

NOTE: Famous for his carousing and his rhymes, it is thought
Elderton fell victim to the bottle in 1592.

My grandfather was buried here,
My cousin Jane, and two uncles dear;
My father perished
with a mortification in his thighs,
My sister dropped down dead in the Minories.
But the reason why I am here,
according to my thinking,
Is owing to my good living and hard drinking,
Therefore good Christians,
if you'd wish to live long,
Beware of drinking brandy, gin,
or anything strong.

Thetford, Norfolk

A PAIR OF MISERS

Reader, beware, immoderate love of pelf,
Here lies the worst of thieves —
who robb'd himself.

Frome churchyard, Somerset

Here lyeth father Sparges
That dyed to save charges.

ROBERT COX
(DIED IN 1666)

Lewd did I live
Evil did I dwell.

St Laurence, Warborough, Oxfordshire

ON A LOOSE-LIVING VICAR

He was literally a father
to all the children of the parish.

(18th century)

Here lie the bones of Elizabeth Charlotte
Born a virgin, died a harlot.
She was aye a virgin at seventeen
A remarkable thing in Aberdeen.

Mr Pricke

Upon the fifth day of November
Christ's College lost a privy member;
Cupid and death did both their arrows nick,
Cupid shot short, but death did hit the prick;
Women lament and maidens make great moans,
Because the prick is laid beneath the stones.

Here lies a lewd Fellow, who,
while he drew Breath,
In the Midst of his Life was in Quest of his Death;
Which he quickly obtain'd for it cost him his Life,
For being in Bed with another Man's Wife.

NOTE: This epitaph was written by John Bowden of Chester,
a professional writer of epitaphs, who published The
Epitaph-Writer in 1791, with 600 suggested verses.

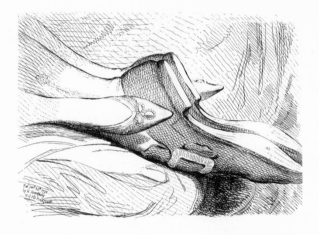

**CLAUDE DU VALL, HIGHWAYMAN, HANGED AT TYBURN
(1643—70)**

Here lies Du Vall: Reader, if male thou art,
Look to thy purse, if female, to thy heart.
Much havock has he made of both; for all
Men he made stand, and women he made fall ...

St Paul's churchyard, Covent Garden, London

Here lies the body of William Smith;
   and, what is somewhat rarish:
He was born, bred and hanged in this parish.

Penryn, Cornwall

**COLEMAN, A PLOTTING PAPIST,
DURING THE REIGN OF CHARLES II**

If heav'n be pleas'd, when sinners cease to sin;
   If hell be please'd, when sinners enter in;
   If earth be pleas'd, when ridded of a knave;
Then all are pleas'd — for COLEMAN'S in his grave.

MARTIN MAR, PRELATE

The Welshman is hanged,
   Who at our kirk flanged,
   And her state banged,
   And breaded are his bukes;
   And though he be hanged,
   Yet he is not wranged,
   The devil has him fanged,
   In his cruked klukes.

ROBIN PEMBERTON

Here lies ROBIN but not ROBIN HOOD;
Here lies ROBIN that never did good;
Here lies ROBIN by heav'n forsaken;
Here lies ROBIN — the Devil may take un.

South Shields, Tyne and Wear

Here fast asleep lies SAUNDERS SCOTT,
Long may he snort and snore;
His bains are now in GORMAN'S pot,
That us'd to strut the streets before.

He liv'd a lude and tastrel life,
For gude he nae regarded;
His perjur'd clack rais'd mickle strife,
For whilk belike he'll be rewarded ...

Traditional Scottish epitaph

T'ill Death Do Us Part

TILL DEATH DO US PART

Here lyeth the body of
WILLIAM STRUTTON, of Patrington,
Buried the 18th of May 1734
Aged 97.
Who had, by his first wife,
twenty-eight children,
And by a second seventeen;
Own father to forty-five
Grand-father to eighty-six
Great Grand-father to ninety-seven,
And Great, Great Grand-father
to twenty-three;
In all two hundred and fifty-one.

Hedon, Holderness, East Yorkshire

Here lies the body of
ELIZABETH,
Wife of
MAJOR GENERAL HAMILTON,
Who was married forty-seven years,
And never did one thing
to disoblige her husband.
She died 18th March, 1746.

Streatham churchyard, London

Here lies the wife of Roger Martin;
She was a good wife to Roger,
that's quite sartin.

Walworth, County Durham

WIFE OF SIR ALBERT MORTON

He first deceased; she for a little tried
To live without him, liked it not, and died.

(16th century)

I am anxiously expecting you — AD 1827
Here I am. — AD 1867

Paris, France

Here lies the body of Mary Ford,
Whose soul, we hope, is with the Lord;
But if for hell she's changed this life,
It's better than being John Ford's wife.

Upton-on-Severn, Worcestershire

ON A SCOLDING WIFE
WHO DIED IN HER SLEEP

Here lies the quintessence
of noise and strife,
Or, in one word,
here lies a scolding wife;
Had not death took her
when her mouth was shut,
He durst not for his ears
have touch'd the slut.

Here lies by wife POLLY, a terrible shrew;
If I said I was sorry, I should lie too.

Australia

Here lies my poor wife,
without bed or blanket,
But dead as a door-nail,
God be thankèd.

Yorkshire

Painful Ends

Here lie the remains of
THOMAS LAMB,
killed by a great big tree
falling upon him, slap bang.

Prince Edward's Island, Canada

Here doth lye the bodie
Of John Flye, who did die
By a stroke from a sky-rocket
Which hit on the eye-socket.

Durness churchyard, Sutherlandshire

Here lies JOHN ROSS,
Kicked by a hoss.

Jersey

Here lie I,
and no wonder I'm dead,
For the wheel of a waggon
went over my head.

Pembrokeshire

Wheel

ON A CLERK'S SON, KILLED BY A FALLING ICICLE, 1776

By my i i i i
Here he lies
In a sad pickle
Kill'd by an icicle.

Bampton, Devon

Here lies entombed one Roger Morton,
Whose sudden death was early brought on;
Trying one day his corn to mow off,
The razor slipped and cut his toe off:

The toe, or rather what it grew to,
An inflammation quickly flew to;
The parts they took to mortifying,
And poor dear Roger took to dying.

Acton churchyard, Cornwall

ON MRS ANN FARLAM,
WHO DIED BY THE BITE
OF HER FAVOURITE LAP DOG

Death, the last end of all, is fix'd, is sure,
But manifold the means that end procure.
My little favourite cur, my guiltless friend,
Thy tooth with frenzy struck, induc'd my end.
Be ready, mortals, for the solemn call;
No matter what the means by which you fall.

Chatham churchyard, Kent

Cur

SIR CHARLES ROSE
(DIED 1913)

From the effects
of an aeroplane flight.

He was young
He was fair
But the Injuns
Raised his hair.

Colorado

ON A MAN WHO WAS
SCALDED TO DEATH

Sacred to the memory
of our 'steamed friend.

New Orleans

Here lies the body of our Anna
Done to death by a banana
It wasn't the fruit that laid her low
But the skin of the thing that made her go.

Ithaca, New York

SweetPowder.

Here lies the body of Mary Ann Lowder,
She burst while drinking a seidleitz powder,
Called from this world to her heavenly rest,
She should have waited 'till it effervesced.

Burlington, New Jersey, 1798

He got a fish-bone in his throat,
And then he sang an angel note.

Schenectady, New York

DONALD ROBERTSON
(1785—1848)

Here lies I and my three daughters.
Killed by a drinking of the Cheltenham waters;
If we had stuck to Epsom salts,
We'd not been a lying in these vaults.

Cheltenham, Gloucestershire

MARY, SARAH AND
ELIZA ATWOOD
(1794—1808, 1801—8
AND 1803—8)

Mary, Sarah and
Eliza Atwood
who were poisoned by
eating fungous vegetables
mistaken for champignons
on the 11th day of October 1808
and died at the ages of 14, 7 and 5 years
within a few hours of each other
in excruciating circumstances.
The father, mother and now,
alas, an only child,
partakers of the same meal,
have survived with debilitated
constitutions and to lament
so dreadful a calumny.
This monument is erected
to perpetuate the fatal events
as an awful caution to others,
let it be too
a solemn warning that in our most grateful
enjoyments even in our necessary food
may lurk deadly poison.

25   26   27   28

My father and mother
were both insane
I inherited the terrible stain.
My grandfather, grandmother,
aunts and uncles
Were lunatics all,
and yet died of carbuncles.

Maryland

Here lies buried in this tomb
A constant sufferer from salt rheum,
Which finally in truth did pass
To spotted erysipelas.
A husband brave, a father true,
Here he lies, and so must you.

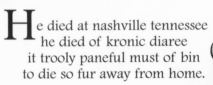

Baton Rouge, Louisiana

He died at nashville tennessee
he died of kronic diaree
it trooly paneful must of bin
to die so fur away from home.

Indiana

Under this marble fair
Lies the body entomb'd of Gervase Aire;
He dyd not of an ague fit,
Not surfeited by too much wit:
Methinks this was a wondrous death,
That Aire should die for want of breath.

St Giles, Cripplegate, London

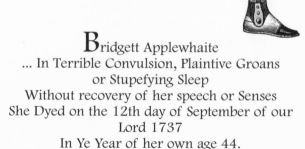

Poor Martha Snell!
her's gone away,
Her would if her could,
but her couldn't stay;
Her'd two sore legs,
and a baddish cough,
But her legs it was
as carried her off.

Staverton churchyard, Devon

Bridgett Applewhaite
... In Terrible Convulsion, Plaintive Groans
or Stupefying Sleep
Without recovery of her speech or Senses
She Dyed on the 12th day of September of our
Lord 1737
In Ye Year of her own age 44.

Bramfield Parish Church, Suffolk

Untimely Ends

(EX UTERO STATIM TRANSLATUS EST AD TUMULUM)

To Joanni MAGIO,
An incomparable boy,
Who, thro' the unskilfulness
of the Midwife,
On the 21st day of December, 1532,
Was translated from the womb to the tomb.

Venice

ON A TWO-WEEK OLD BABY

Came in,
Looked about;
Didn't like it
Went out.

Suffolk

Beneath this stone
        our baby lays
He neither cries
        nor hollers;
He lived just one
        and twenty days
And cost us forty dollars.

Burlington, Iowa

ON AN INFANT ONLY THREE MONTHS OLD

SINCE I am so quickly done for,
I wonder what I was begun for.

Cheltenham, Gloucestershire

Here lie two babbies, as dead as nits,
        Who died in agonizing fits;
They were too good to live with we,
So God did take to live with He.

Gloucestershire

MARIA SCOTT
(DIED APRIL 1836, AGED 7)

The cup of life just with her lips she prest,
Found the taste bitter, and declin'd the rest.
Averse: then turning from the face of day,
She softly sighed her little soul away.

Ely Cathedral churchyard, Cambridgeshire

To the memory of Emma
and Maria Littleboy,
The twin children of
George and Emma
Littleboy, of Hornsey,
who died July 16th, 1783.
Two Littleboys lie here,
yet strange to say these
Littleboys are girls.

Hornsey churchyard, London

JERRY HOWELLS

Death has taken little Jerry,
Son of Joseph and Serena Howells;
Seven days did he wrestle with the dystentery,
Then he perished in his little bowels.

(18th century)

JULIA ADAMS

Died of thin shoes
April 17th, 1838, aged 19 years.

New Jersey

In memory of Jane Bent,
Who kick'd up her heels
and away she went.

Rochville, Eastern Massachusetts

NOTE: There is a similar inscription for
Jane Kitchen in Bury St Edmunds, Suffolk:

Here lies Jane Kitchen, who,
when her glass was spent,
Kickt up her heels and away she went.

Grim death took me
without any warning,
I was well at night,
and dead at nine
in the morning.

Sevenoaks, Kent

Not Much Missed

NOT MUCH MISSED

Beneath this stone and not above it
Lie the remains of Anna Lovett.
Be pleased, dear reader, not to shove it
For 'twixt you and I, no one does covet
To see again this Anna Lovett.
Left us May 17th, 1769.

New England

Molly, tho' pleasant in her day
Was suddenly seized and sent away.
How soon she's ripe, how soon she's rotten,
Laid in the grave and soon forgetten.

Milford, Connecticut, 1792

Poor John Thomas,
here he lies;
No one laughs,
no one cries;
Where he's gone
and how he fares,
No one knows,
and no one cares.

Ash churchyard

46

JEMIMA JONES
(DIED 1803)

This is the last long resting place
of Aunt Jemima Jones
Her soul ascended into space
Amidst our tears and groans
She was not pleasing to the eye
Nor had she any brain
And when she talked twas through her nose
Which gave her friends much pain
But still we feel that she was worth
The money that was spent
Upon the coffin, hearse and stone
(The funeral plumes were lent).

ON A CHEATING GAMBLER

Here lies the clay of
Mitchell Coots,
Whose feet yet occupy his boots.
His soul has gone — we know not where
It landed, neither do we care ...

Lost Creek, Colorado

Short and Sweet

Finis Maginnis

Ireland

**RICHARD BURBAGE, SHAKESPEARIAN ACTOR
(1567—1619)**

Exit Burbage.

ON AN AUCTIONEER

Going, Going, Gone.

Greenwood, New York

TO THE MEMORY OF STEPHEN SMITH, ORGANIST

Stephen and time
are now both even,
Stephen beat time,
but now time
has beat Stephen.

St Mark's, Yorkshire

DR J. J. SUBERS
(DIED 1916, AGED 78)

Been Here
and Gone
Had a Good Time

Rosehill churchyard, Macon, Georgia

DR FULLER, THE CELEBRATED DIVINE,
Here lies Fuller's Earth.

ON A WORKHOUSE PAUPER
(THE PARISH SPENT AS LITTLE AS POSSIBLE
ON HIS INSCRIPTION)

Thorpe's
Corpse.

Here lies John Yeast.
Pardon me for not rising.

Ruidoso, New Mexico

Professional to the End

SAMUEL FOOTE, COMEDIAN
(1720—77)

Here lies one Foote,
whose death may thousands save,
For death has now one foot within the grave.

Westminster Abbey, London

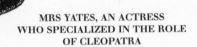

MRS YATES, AN ACTRESS
WHO SPECIALIZED IN THE ROLE
OF CLEOPATRA

No more our fancy 'wails the tragic Queen,
For Heaven has verified the DYING SCENE.

WALLACE FORD, BRITISH ACTOR
(1897—1966)

At last I get top billing.

SIR NOEL COWARD
(1899—1973)

A talent to amuse.

ON A FEISTY SCOTTISH LASS

Fair Maiden LILLYARD lies under this stane,
Little was her stature,
but great was her fame;
Upon the English louns she laid mony thumps,
And when her legs were cutted off,
she fought upon her stumps.

NOTE: The Battle of Lillyard's Edge was fought in 1545.
Tradition says that a beautiful young Scottish girl,
Lillyard, followed her lover to the fray and, when
he fell, she herself rushed in to battle, and
was killed — but not before slaying several
of the English enemy.

ON A LIVERPOOL BREWER

Poor JOHN SCOTT lies buried here;
Although he was both hale and stout
Death stretched him on the bitter bier.
In another world he hops about.

ON A COALHEAVER

Cease To Lament His Change, Ye Just,
He's Only Gone From Dust To Dust.

Here lies John Higgs,
A famous man for killing pigs,
For killing pigs was his delight
Both morning, afternoon, and night.
Both heats and cold he did endure,
Which no physician could ere cure.
His knife is laid, his work is done;
I hope to Heaven his soul has gone.

Cheltenham, Gloucestershire

52

Here lies, in horizontal position,
the outside case of
GEORGE ROUTLEIGH, Watchmaker;
Whose abilities in that line
were an honour to his profession.
Integrity was the Mainspring,
and prudence the Regulator,
of all the actions of his life.
Humane, generous, and liberal,
his Hand never stopped
till he had relieved distress.
So nicely regulated were all his motions,
that he never went wrong,
except when set a-going
by people who did not know his Key;
even then he was easily set right again.
He had the art of disposing his time so well,
that his hours glided away
in one continual round
of pleasure and delight,
until an unlucky minute put
a period to his existence.
He departed this life
November 14th, 1802,
aged 57, wound up,
in hopes of being taken
in hand by his Maker;

Clock-work.

and of being thoroughly cleaned,
repaired, and set a-going
in the world to come.

Lydford churchyard, Dartmoor

Here lie the remains of James Pady,
Brickmaker, late of the parish,
in hopes that his clay may be remoulded
in a workmanlike manner, far superior
to his former perishable materials.
Keep death and Judgement always in your eye,
Or else the devil off with you will fly,
And in his kiln with brimstone ever fry.
If you neglect the narrow road to seek,
Christ will reject you, like a half Burnt Brick.

Wiveliscombe, Devon

ROBERT TROLLOPE,
ARCHITECT OF THE EXCHANGE
AND GUILDHALL IN NEWCASTLE

Here lies Robert Trollope
Who made yon stones roll up:
When death took his soul up,
His body fill'd this hole up.

Gateshead, Tyne and Wear

ON A YORKSHIRE COOK
OR NELL BATCHELOR THE OXFORD PIE-WOMAN

Underneath this crust
Lies the mouldering dust
Of ELEANOR BATCHELOR SHOVEN,
Well versed in the Arts
Of pies, custards, and tarts,
And the lucrative trade of the oven.
When she lived long enough
She made her last puff,
A puff by her husband much praised,
And now she doth lie
And make a dirt pie,
In hopes that her crust may be raised.

The body of
BENJAMIN FRANKLIN,
Printer
Like the cover of an old book,
Its contents torn out,
And stript of its lettering and gilding,
Lies here, food for worms.
But the work itself shall not be lost,
For it will, as he believed, appear once more,
In a new and more elegant edition,
Revised and corrected
By
The Author.

NOTE: Benjamin Franklin's own epitaph for himself was based on
that of Jacob Tonson, who died in 1735. The epitaph, by an Eton scholar,
was printed in the Gentleman's Magazine, February 1736. The famous
Franklin epitaph was not used on his grave, which bears simply the
name of his wife, and the date 1790. It is to be found in the cemetery
of Christ Church, Philadelphia.

MR EDMOND PURDON, AUTHOR

Here lies poor Ned Purdon, from misery freed,
Who long was a bookseller's hack,
He led such a damnable life in this world,
I don't think he'll ever come back.

ADAM WILLIAMSON,
PRESSMAN-PRINTER, IN EDINBURGH,
WHO DIED OCTOBER 3RD, 1832, AGED 72 YEARS

My spindle and bar have lost their power;
My till is laid aside;
Both legs of my crane are turned out of their path;
My platen can make no impression;
My winter hath no spring;
My rounce will neither roll out nor in;
Stone, coffin and carriage have all failed;
The hinges of my tympan and frisket
are immovable;
My long and short ribs are rusted;
My cheeks are much worm-eaten
and mouldering away:
My press is totally down:
The volume of my life is finished,
Not without many errors;
Most of them have arisen from bad composition,
and are to be attributed more
to the chase than the press;
There are also a great number of my own;
Misses, scuffs, blotches, blurs, and bad register;
But the true and faithful Superintendent has
undertaken to correct the whole.
When the machine is again set up
(incapable of decay),
A new and perfect edition of my life will appear,
Elegantly bound for duration, and every way fitted
for the grand Library of the Great Author.

NOTE: All the puns above refer to the operation of the
old wooden press for printing.

57

SIR JOHN STRANGE
(1696—1754)

Here lies an honest lawyer,
— That is Strange.

Here lies a Lawyer,
sold each blast of breath,
Till at the Bar he bawl'd himself to Death.

NOTE: In this letter "The Female Critick" suggests that her
unwanted suitor, the lawyer, should have his own skin shaved off
by the Scrivener, in order to make a parchment to bear this
inscription for his epitaph.
from The Female Critick, or, LETTERS in Drollery from
LADIES to their humble Servants

JOHN SHAW, ATTORNEY

Here lies John Shaw
Attorney-at-law;
And when he died,
The Devil cried,
"Give us your paw,
John Shaw,
Attorney-at-law!"
"Pshaw! pshaw!"

WILLIAM WILSON, A TROUBLESOME LITIGANT

Here lieth W. W.
Who never more will trouble you, trouble you.

Lambeth churchyard, London

59

Major
Born a dog
Died a Gentleman.

Aspin Hill Cemetery for Pets,
Aspen, Maryland

**LORD BYRON'S INSCRIPTION
ON THE MONUMENT OF HIS DOG**

Near this spot
Are deposited the remains of one
Who possessed beauty without vanity,
Strength without insolence,
Courage without ferocity,
And all the virtues of man without his vices,
This praise, which would be unmeaning flattery,
If inscribed over human ashes,
Is but a just tribute to the memory of
BOATSWAIN, a dog,
Who was born at Newfoundland, May 1803,
And died at Newstead Abbey,
November 18th, 1808.

Passer-by, contemplate here
the mortal remains of THE PIG,
which acquired for itself imperishable glory,
by the discovery
of the Salt Springs of Luneburg.

Inscription on a monument of black marble at the Hotel de Ville,
Luneburg, Hanover, Germany

In profound appreciation
of the Boll Weevil and what it has done
as the herald of prosperity.
This monument was erected by the citizens of
Enterprise, Coffee County, Alabama.

NOTE: The spread of this pest in America from 1915 onwards
forced the southern Cotton Belt states to diversify into other crops
such as corn and peanuts, which produced wealth and success for
many. In 1919 a monumental fountain was erected in Enterprise
with the above inscription.

**MAGGIE, AN ARMY MULE IN FRANCE
DURING THE SECOND WORLD WAR**

In memory of MAGGIE
who in her time kicked
Two colonels, Four majors,
Ten captains,
Twenty-four lieutenants,
Forty-two sergeants,
Four hundred and
thirty-two other ranks
AND One Mills Bomb.

The Grateful Dead

CATHERINE ALSOPP
(HANGED HERSELF IN 1905)

Here lies a poor woman who always was tired,
For she lived in a place where help wasn't hired,
Her last words on earth were,
"Dear friends, I am going,
Where washing ain't done nor cooking nor sewing,
And everything there is exact to my wishes,
For there they don't eat, there's no washing of dishes,
I'll be where loud anthems will always be ringing
(But having no voice, I'll be out of the singing).
Don't mourn for me now, don't grieve for me never,
For I'm going to do nothing for ever and ever."

Sheffield, South Yorkshire

ON AN INVALID WRITTEN BY HIMSELF

Here lies a head that often ached;
Here lie two hands that always shak'd;
Here lies a brain of odd conceit;
Here lies a heart that often beat;
Here lie two eyes that dimly wept,
And in the night but seldom slept;
Here lies a tongue that whining talk'd;
Here lie two feet that feebly walked;
Here lie the midriff and the breast,
With loads of indigestion prest;
Here lies the liver, full of bile,
That ne'er secreted proper chyle;
Here lie the bowels, human tripes,
Tortured with wind and twisting gripes;
Here lies the livid dab, the spleen,
The source of life's sad tragic scene,
That left side weight that clogs the blood,
And stagnates Nature's circling flood;
Here lies the back, oft racked with pains,
Corroding kidneys, loins, and reins;
Here lies the skin by scurvy fed,
With pimples and irruptions red;
Here lies the man from top to toe,
That fabric fram'd for pain and woe.

The Great Hereafter

Sacred to the memory of inestimable worth of unrivalled excellence and virtue, N. R., whose ethereal parts became seraphic May 25th, 1767.

Litchfield, Connecticut

ON A LADY WHO KEPT AN
EARTHENWARE SHOP AT CHESTER

Beneath this stone lies CATHERINE GRAY,
Changed to a lifeless lump of clay;
By earth and clay she got her pelf,
And now she's turned to earth herself.
Ye weeping friends, let me advise,
Abate your tears and dry your eyes;
For what avails a flood of tears?
Who knows but in a course of years,
In some tall pitcher or brown pan,
She in her shop may be again?

JOYCE RICH DIED AUGUST 1679, AGED 74; ALSO
ELIZABETH WINTER, HER DAUGHTER, WHO DIED
IN THE LORD, NOVEMBER 9TH, 1687, AGED 47.

We two within this grave do lye,
Where we do rest together;
Until the Lord shall us awake,
And from the goats us sever.

Stepney, London